Spiritual Lessons

from a Scam

Alexander and Eva Peck

© 2022 by Alexander and Eva Peck

All rights reserved
Except for any fair dealing permitted under the Copyright Act, no part of this book may be reproduced by any means without prior permission of the author and publisher.

Bible quotes, unless otherwise indicated, are taken from the *Holy Bible, New International Version*. Copyright © 1973, 1978, 1984 by International Bible Society. Used by permission of Zondervan Publishing House. All rights reserved.

Graphic design and preparation for publishing: Eva Peck
Cover design: Eva Peck

Photography
Cover photo: Eva Peck
Author photo: Waitress at a restaurant

ISBN: 978-0-9876279-4-0

A catalogue record for this book is available from the National Library of Australia

The book can be purchased online through:
www.pathway-publishing.org, Amazon and other outlets.

Pathway Publishing
Seeking truth and beauty

Dedicated to God, or the Source of All Things,
who has always supplied our needs;
and to those who have been hurt
by unscrupulous scams.

Other Spiritual Books by the Authors

Eva Peck

Divine Reflections in Times and Seasons

Divine Reflections in Natural Phenomena

Divine Reflections in Living Things

Divine Insights from Human Life

Jesus' Gospel of God's Love

New Birth – Pathway to the Kingdom of God

Gospel of God's Grace and His Kingdom

Abundant Living on Low Income

Alex and Eva Peck

Pathway to Life – Through the Holy Scriptures

Journey to the Divine within – Through Silence, Stillness and Simplicity

Realities of Life – Reflections in Verse

See also
www.pathway-publishing.org

Acknowledgments

First, I would like to thank God, the Source of All Things for enabling, inspiring, and blessing the publication of this book. Even though it was born out of the trial and trauma of a scam, I am grateful for all the help received and insights gained, and the resulting spiritual growth and transformation.

I must thank my husband, Alex, for his sizeable and valuable involvement in this book through researching and contributing information, as well as helpful editorial suggestions. While we both shared in the challenging experience of financial loss through a scam, we also traversed together the healing process and thus were able to support and encourage each other, as well as pooling our insights.

Finally, I am grateful that the trial and trauma were not more than we could bear, that our loss did not affect our livelihood, and that we now have much more compassion for the countless others who too have been unsuspectingly caught in various scams. I am also thankful that through our experience, we may be able to help others similarly affected.

Eva Peck
December 2022

Contents

Preface 1

Introduction 3

Anatomy of a Scam 6

Aftermath of Being Scammed 8

Practical Tips 10

    Alertness and Watchfulness 10
    Healthy Suspicion 10
    Discernment 11
    Ten Golden Rules of Protection 11

Health 16

    Sleep and Rest 16
    Diet 16
    Exercise 18
    Mental Health 21

Spiritual Lessons and Insights 24

    Seeking First the Kingdom of God 24
    Prayer and Spiritual Focus 27
    Faith in God 29
    Acceptance 31
    Focus on the Positive 38
    Gratitude 41
    Preciousness Time 44
    Eight Worldly Concerns 48
    Love of Money 52

- Generosity 54
- Cause and Effect (Karma) 58
- Mindfulness 62
- Compassion 68
- Forgiveness 72

The Peace Method 77

- Present Moment 77
- Expressing Feelings 78
- Acceptance and Appreciation 78
- Considering the Contrary 79
- Enthusiasm 80

Loving One's Enemies 81

Prayers 87

- Prayers for Ourselves and the Scammers 87
- Prayer from a Different Perspective 90

Afterword 93

About the Authors 98

- Eva Peck 98
- Alexander Peck 99

About Pathway Publishing 101

Preface

The purpose of this book is to help those who have been victims of scams or other crimes resulting in loss and trauma, as well as the turbulent emotions of grief, anger, desire for revenge, denial, depression, helplessness, hopelessness, and despair.

The insights are an outgrowth of our experience of being scammed and left wondering how on earth could we have fallen for something like that. It is also our healing journey from darkness to light.

For us, reviewing and applying the principles in this book has resulted in spiritual growth. It has also spawned compassion for the countless other victims of scams. Compassion is equally needed for the perpetrators, for in due time, even if it is in the next life, they will reap what they have sown, and experience the pain that they have inflicted on their victims — unless they have turned from their ways with deep regret and remorse over their actions.

The book is not intended to provide comprehensive information on how to avoid scams, which nowadays is readily available. While it does contain basic practical tips, its focus is on spiritual principles. These come mainly from two spiritual traditions – Christianity (supplied by Eva) and Buddhism (supplied by Alex).

The spiritual principles from both traditions can help facilitate healing by reorienting the mind from dwelling on the pain, loss, helplessness, desire for revenge, anger, hate, and similar thoughts and emotions to higher perspectives of understanding, forgiveness, gratitude, compassion, and ultimately love, all of which are life-giving and health-conducive.

In the context of suffering, this quote is instructive and relevant: "Heartbreak and hope are not mutually exclusive. We can be angry and sad and filled with longing for something we cannot have, and simultaneously we can be grateful for what we've got — aware, for reasons we'd never choose, of what really matters and what doesn't." (Lennon Flowers)

The ideas and principles in this book have been applied, and are in the process of being applied by the authors and found to be helpful. If consistently and repeatedly put into practice, we believe that they can also help you, the reader, to begin to free yourself from mental and emotional pain and raise your perspective to higher planes of existence.

In closing, may the information shared in this book be of valuable assistance in being protected from a scam and helping those who have been victims of a scam – or suffered other losses and traumas. In addition, may we all discover precious intangibles, which in the long run could far exceed any monetary or physical loss.

So let's begin the journey ...

Introduction

I do not usually answer unknown calls, especially if they are from interstate. That morning, almost as though led into it, I got up from the sofa and picked up our portable handset of the landline phone. Events happened quickly in the conversation – and both my husband and I got hooked and ended up being drawn, where under normal circumstances we would have never ventured.

Regrettably, countless others have fallen victims to financial scams. In fact, more and more people are losing large sums of money through being scammed. As the scammers are becoming cleverer and more sophisticated, yet more people will be caught unawares – unless keeping well informed about scams and constantly vigilant.

The call on that fateful morning came from a lady supposedly from the Security Department of VISA and Master Card of our bank. She asked if I had made two specific transactions on my VISA card earlier that day. When I said no, she said there was other suspicious activity on our account, and transferred me to the Fraud and Detection department (which does exist at the bank). I ended up talking to a woman by the name of Veronica. She said that 74 attempts were made to withdraw money from our accounts during the past week, all traceable to the local bank branch.

Introduction

She asked that, in order to help them catch the perpetrator/s, I go to the bank, withdraw a sum from our account, and deposit it temporarily (for one hour) into a cloud account at the neighbouring bank. At that time, she sounded plausible and convinced us that she was trying to help us and we were helping her. She cleverly swayed my husband and me to trust her, and under the emotion of the moment, we did as she asked. Unfortunately, only later did we realize that she was a fraudster herself, transferring money directly or indirectly from our account to accomplices!

During the interactions with Veronica, she had me download apps for the purpose of gaining access to my computer. She seemed to have known ahead of time what accounts I had – hence her foul motive was not immediately obvious. She said she would call the next day to further work on the matter. Our call ended with reassurances that our money taken out of our account would be restored at the end of the following business day.

Thankfully, by early evening the same day, we caught on what had happened and I reported the scam/fraud to the bank early the next morning – at 3:30 am because I couldn't sleep. They locked access to our internet banking and advised us not to have any further communication with the scammer, so we ignored all the calls – which were numerous.

Introduction

Looking back the next day, both my husband and I couldn't believe that we did what we were asked to do. It was almost like a spell was cast over us. Our emotions were activated and our judgment suspended. Even though we were aware of the existence of scammers and reasonably careful, this one caught us unawares.

Yet, sadly, we are far from alone to whom something of this nature has happened. Millions are being scammed around the world of large amounts of money. Senior citizens especially (which we both are now) are vulnerable to scammers' tactics some of which are described in the next section.

Anatomy of a Scam

This information comes from the webinar entitled "The Neuroscience behind Financial Scams" (https://www.youtube.com/watch?v=ywtlYQ7wEFM).

The webinar is described as follows: "Older Americans lose billions annually to financial scams and experience a range of harms resulting from their victimization. At times our response is incredulous and at times sympathetic. What is nearly universal is a lack of understanding of why older adults fall victim to these scams. Using brain science and psychological principles, Erik Lande, a neuropsychologist, guides attendees through an explanation of the mechanisms that facilitate vulnerability to financial scams." Erik comes to the following conclusions:

Aging disproportionately affects the frontal lobe and prefrontal cortex, which is involved in decision making and judgment – especially the kind of decisions involved in scams. This results in decreased ability to process information in a rapid manner. It also results in increased susceptibility to financial exploitation involving urgency and emotional information. Hence seniors are increasingly vulnerable due to their aging brain.

In addition, physical, emotional and societal issues play a role. Senior adults have trouble holding onto information, they don't think about it, and therefore may act impulsively. This is exacerbated by the visceral nature of scams. They tend to grab a person by the guts and one just tends to go along with the scammer.

Seniors are also disadvantaged by the fact that they are not up-to-date on technological advances and cannot readily discern what a scammer may be up to. They may also have sensory limitations – hearing and sight – and other health issues, as well as feeling lonely, which further makes them vulnerable to being taken advantage of by seemingly friendly callers. In fact, many well-off seniors have lost much of their wealth through being scammed out of it.

Aftermath of Being Scammed

Being financially scammed (as we were) leaves the victim reeling with a range of turbulent emotions including:

Despair – what do I do now? This is especially true if the loss is sizeable, and even more so, if it affects one's livelihood or future.

Guilt, embarrassment and shame – for example, "how dumb of me to have allowed this to happen!" Such thoughts and emotions tend to keep victims in isolation – not wanting to share their suffering with others, or report it to authorities.

If only ... – "if only I did/didn't do ..." Such thinking tends to exacerbate the feelings of guilt and shame.

Anger – "how could they have dared do this to me?" When innocent trust has been betrayed by the scammer, anger toward them can quickly arise.

Denial – "it can't be true!" To realize that a sizeable amount of money has been stealthily taken away is difficult to come to terms with – and will take time to acknowledge and accept.

Fear – could it happen again? It is a sad fact, that once a person has been scammed, unless they are extra vigilant, it could happen again.

Grief with all its associated emotions. Having suffered a financial scam represents a genuine loss.

Therefore, a period of grieving will occur, as happens whenever we experience any substantial loss in life.

Depression – self-pity and sadness, that in extreme cases can be debilitating.

From our personal experience – and undoubtedly true of others in similar situations – waves of emotions can keep one awake at night, and down in the dumps during the day. But the good news is that healing can and does come in due time.

The information that follows has helped us and it is our heartfelt hope that it may help others to re-orient their perspective, learn valuable lessons, and be wiser in the future.

Practical Tips

Here is some information to remain on guard against a possible scam and terminate any suspicious phone call or online relationship before it is too late.

Alertness and Watchfulness

Be alert for warning signs and act immediately to protect yourself. For example:

-- Deny any requests for remote access to your computer.

-- Hang up on people claiming to be from a big and legitimate organization (e.g., bank, telephone company, utilities company, government) and who try to rush you into acting.

-- Discern a person playing on your emotions (e.g., fear) and leading you to make decisions you would not otherwise make.

-- Recognize and put a stop to the manipulation of your trust – gaining it to later betray it.

Healthy Suspicion

While not wanting to believe the worst, be wary of unknown callers, emailers or texters.

-- Don't answer unknown callers – if it is important, they will leave a message and you can decide whether or not to call back.

-- If you do answer, you could consider answering along the following lines: "Thank you for calling. This is not a good time for me. Please redial this number and leave a message if you like. I can call you back later, if I need to. Thanks for your understanding."

-- Don't get hooked into any conversation that may lead into unintended and negative consequences.

-- Don't respond to suspicious emails or messages, but delete them. Above all, do not click on any links – they are often fake and can open you up to having personal information stolen.

Discernment

Realize that as older adults (above 50), we are very vulnerable to scams and deceit. At all times and in all situations, be discerning and discriminating to the best of your ability!

-- Ask questions to be thoroughly informed. Don't let anyone to rush you or make you do what you are not sure about or don't understand.

-- If unsure about a situation, ask for more time to consider all the options.

-- If still in doubt, it is best to leave it!

Ten Golden Rules of Protection

This helpful information has been compiled by Heritage Bank in Australia.

Practical Tips

Be aware that scams exist

When dealing with unknown contacts from people or businesses, always consider the possibility that the approach may be a scam.

Tip: Search online to confirm the contact details before proceeding.

Don't open suspicious texts or emails – delete them

If unsure, verify the identity of the contact through an independent source such as a phone book or online search. Don't use the contact details provided in the message sent to you.

Tip: If you don't know who sent you the text or email, don't open or click on any links. The safest option is to delete it.

Beware of any requests for your details or money

Never send money or give bank card numbers, account details or copies of personal documents to anyone you don't know or trust. Don't agree to transfer money or goods for someone else; money laundering is a criminal offence.

Be careful when shopping online

Beware of offers that seem too good to be true and always use an online shopping service that you know and trust.

Tip: Look for the closed padlock on the website, as this confirms the site is secure. Do your research before you proceed with a site that doesn't have a secure padlock.

Beware of unusual payment methods

Scammers often ask for payment by wire transfers, preloaded cards and even Google Play, Steam, or iTunes gift cards and cryptocurrency. These are nearly always a sign that it is part of a scam.

Tip: Do your research via an independent source before you proceed.

Know who you're dealing with

If you've only ever met someone online or are unsure of the legitimacy of a business, take some time to do a bit more research. Search online for real business photos or for reviews from others who may have had dealings with them. Beware that scammers will try and tell you what to say and how to act to avoid detection. Don't be afraid to ask questions.

Keep your personal details secure

Keep your passwords and PIN (personal ID number) in a safe place and never share them with anyone or write them down. Be very careful about how much personal information you share on social media sites. Scammers can use your information and pictures to create a fake identity or to target you with a scam.

Tip: Never share codes sent to you as an SMS from the bank to anyone – not even the bank.

Keep your mobile devices and computers secure

Always use password protection, don't share access to your computer or phone with anyone (including remotely), update security software and back up content regularly. Protect your WiFi network with a password and avoid using public computers or WiFi hotspots to access online banking or provide personal information. If you are not sure how to do this, ask a trusted individual for assistance.

Choose your passwords carefully

Choose passwords that would be difficult for others to guess and update them regularly. A strong password should include a mix of upper- and lower-case letters, numbers and symbols (try a phrase). Don't use the same password for every account/profile, and don't share your passwords with anyone.

If you have concerns, contact your bank immediately or visit your nearest branch.

Source: https://www.heritage.com.au/support/security-alerts.

Practical Tips

The previously mentioned website allows visitors to download the pamphlet entitled "The golden rules to protect yourself from scams and fraud." It is an excellent resource. See the section entitled "Scam alerts & fraud protection" for its wide range of help guides and security tips. We heartily recommend this trusted website.

Other tips can be found on this website:
https://www.scamwatch.gov.au/get-help/where-to-get-help#toc-report-scams-to-the-authorities

Health

Health is important to be able to remain on guard against scammers. In fact, health issues and impaired abilities are what increases one's chances to become a scam victim. Below are a few practices that will help maintain good physical and mental health.

Sleep and Rest

Getting enough sleep and rest each day is one of the most important things we can do for our health and well-being.

Sleeping well – and resting when needed – makes us feel better, be more alert and energetic, as well as better able to concentrate and perform our daily tasks. The ability to think sharply can reduce the risk of being caught off-guard by a scam.

In a nutshell, we each need to get sufficient sleep – 7-8 hours, and possibly more with aging – which will help us in sound thinking, judgment and discernment, thereby being more alert for any possible scam approach.

Diet

Our brain needs a lot of nutrients to function and keep us well. Healthy eating helps reduce the risk of physical issues like heart disease and diabetes. It also helps with sleeping patterns, energy levels, and our general health – enabling us to better cope with the stresses of daily life, and spot any potential scams.

Our mood often affects the types of food we choose, as well as how much we eat. We also need to be aware how some foods lift our mood, energy levels and concentration, while others can have the opposite effect. For example, eating lots of fresh fruits, vegetables, nuts, and whole grains can reduce our risk of some mental health conditions such as depression, while foods that are high in sugar and saturated fat may increase that risk.

If we are struggling with ensuring a healthy, balanced diet, our GP can refer us to an Accredited Practising Dietitian (APD) who can provide face-to-face support. Getting in touch with other people who have had challenges with healthy eating may also give us ideas on how to improve our eating habits.

In summary, we need to watch our diet and ensure that it is balanced, adequate, and nutritious, containing all the elements important for good health. This, too, will aid sound judgment and discernment – and optimize our ability to spot any scamming approach before falling headlong into a scam trap.

(Reference: https://www.headtohealth.gov.au/meaningful-life/physical-health/food)

Exercise

Taking good care of our body through sufficient exercise is one of the most important things we can do to improve our mental well-being – and thereby avoid falling prey to any devious scam manoeuvres.

Described below are physical activities that one can do – selecting two or three activities each day.

Give yoga a go

Yoga focuses on strength, flexibility and breathing to boost one's physical and mental well-being. Find a free online video and try it for yourself.

Stand up more

Look for opportunities in your day to stand up, instead of sitting. If you work in an office, consider switching to a standing desk.

Just dance

Dancing combines all the benefits of listening to music and exercising. It is an enjoyable way to be physically active and is suitable for people of all ages and fitness levels.

Join a free exercise class

There are a lot of free online classes and workouts you can do from the comfort of your home. To add intensity or build strength, try using items around the home as weights.

Look for ways to get active
Be creative with how you stay active. Try walking around whenever you are on the phone and move between TV ad breaks or episodes. Increasing your incidental exercise will help you keep active and feeling good.

Try outdoor exercise
Exercising in natural environments can have positive effects on one's mood and self-esteem.

Take a lunchtime walk
Break up your day with a walk at lunchtime. The fresh air and exercise will get the blood and oxygen pumping, which can help improve your focus.

Join a walking group
Walking in a group can help reduce stress and build connections with others in the community. Find a walking group near you.

Take a dog for a walk
Take a dog for a walk and see how it responds to nature. If you don't have your own dog, offer to walk your friend's or neighbour's dog.

Try an outdoor gym
You may find free exercise equipment in parks and community places. If so, jump on and give it a go.

Take a hike

Get moving and enjoy the serenity of the natural world with a hike in the great outdoors. There are tracks to suit every fitness level. Your body and mind will thank you for the fresh air and physical exercise.

(Ref.: https://mentalwellbeing.initiatives.qld.gov.au/)

In sum, as much as possible, ensure adequate exercise each day, or at least five days a week for mental well-being – and thereby remaining more attentive, aware and alert.

For seniors, good forms of exercise include walking, bouncing on a rebounder (mini trampoline), swimming, calisthenics, qigong, or tai chi.

Finally, we all need to be mindful of how we carry ourselves – in other words, our posture. This includes standing or sitting straight, keeping our head level, relaxing our shoulders, and spreading our weight evenly on both legs.

Good posture helps to bring mental composure and an increase in confidence and alertness. Poor posture can lead to lower self-esteem and decreased energy levels. For example, an upright seated posture in the face of stress can maintain self-esteem, reduce negative mood, and increase positiveness compared to a slumped posture.

Mental Health

Being robbed of a sizeable sum of money – with little recourse of getting it back, despite the best efforts of authorities – will affect one mentally. At such time – and at all other times – maintaining one's mental health is critically important.

In our community, the office of a local Member of Parliament has thoughtfully provided a pamphlet entitled "Mental Health Matters". The information shared in this section comes from this publication.

Your mental well-being is the unique way that you handle your emotions, respond to stress, and also your general outlook on life.

A sense of mental well-being has many benefits. It lifts your mood, promotes resilience in difficult situations, and helps you get the most out of life. Taking a few moments for yourself each day to promote this will help you be happier and more resilient. Here are six strategies:

Get healthy – be active, eat well, and get enough sleep.

Keep learning – challenge your mind and seek out new things.

Show kindness – give back, show gratitude, and bring joy to others' lives.

Connect more – develop relationships, stay connected, and care for others.

Take notice – be mindful, stay in the moment. Experience the world around you.

Embrace nature – step outside, connect with nature, and care for the planet.

If you feel that you need help – especially in recovering from a serious scam situation – you can consider:

-- Talking to someone you trust.

-- Seeing your doctor, a counsellor, psychologist, or psychiatrist.

-- Visiting a hospital emergency department.

Sometimes, you might need additional help to feel better again. It's normal to feel sad or worried at times, especially when life gets tough – and it certainly can after a nasty scam and in many other situations.

If you're struggling with your mind, support is available. There are a range of services and organisations that can help you. The below websites are valuable avenues of support in Australia.

https://mentalwellbeing.initiatives.qld.gov.au/

https://www.healthdirect.gov.au/

https://www.lifeline.org.au/

https://headspace.org.au/

https://www.beyondblue.org.au/

https://www.sane.org/

https://www.suicidepreventionaust.org/

Health

https://www.blackdoginstitute.org.au/
https://kidshelpline.com.au/

(Source: Office of Kim Richards, MP. "Mental Health Matters")

Spiritual Lessons and Insights

This section consists of fourteen spiritual lessons and insights that we believe will help those victimized by a scam, or any other crime for that matter, rise above the negative situation, become better people, and be able to move on with life, reaching greater heights.

Seeking First the Kingdom of God

Thich Nhat Hanh, well-known Buddhist teacher and writer, recently deceased, stated:

"Almost all faiths contain the idea of dwelling in a spiritual realm. In Judaism and Christianity, there is the Kingdom of God (Heaven), as well as the Garden of Eden. In Psalms 84, arriving in the Kingdom of God is compared with coming home, 'as the sparrow has found its home at last.'

In Hinduism, there is the abode of the undying, *Amaravati*, presided over by the god Indra. There is also the *Brahma loka* and the *Brahmavihara* (Abode of Brahma) where Hindus aspire to dwell with Brahma. True love can be found here in terms of *maitri* (loving kindness), *karuna* (compassion), *mudita* (joy), and *upeksha* (equanimity).

And in the Qur'an, Eden is also a paradise and there are descriptions of gardens of delight where those who practice their spiritual path dwell close to Allah. According to some, they may even be able to see the face of Allah."

Thich Nhat Hanh further points out how in Buddhism, there is the teaching of Nirvana, and the Pure Land.

Some people believe that the Kingdom of God is only available after we have passed away. According to this teaching, if we sincerely practice our faith and do good deeds in this life, we will reap the benefits sometime in the future, after we have died.

Others, however, realise that the Kingdom of God can be a living reality – to be experienced right here and now. They are aware of living every moment firmly established in the Kingdom of God. This is practicing the highest level of our faith. Such people are able to maintain their constant awareness of the Kingdom of God and all its wholesome qualities.

(Based on Thich Nhat Hanh, *Finding Our True Home: Living in the Pure Land Here and Now*. Berkeley, CA: Parallax Press, 2003)

How then is it possible to experience the Kingdom of God in this life? Those living at the highest level of faith recognize that God is love, and that they can imbibe of His divine love — if they seek to do so. Having the gift of divine love in one's soul is like truly coming home — it is as if we are understanding for the first time the mystery of the ages. Finally, we can begin to fulfil our incredible human potential —

becoming redeemed children of God transformed by His love from being created in only a divine image into a new creature – a divine being. And we do not have to wait until we die!

Living at the highest level of faith includes practicing our faith sincerely and doing good deeds in this life.

When we reflect on the reality of our life, we may discern two realities. First, there is the conventional or relative reality – our physical life and what it entails. Second, there is the ultimate reality – the Kingdom of God.

Jesus encouraged his followers to "seek first the Kingdom of God" — not in the future, but in the present. This precious reality can be experienced now, as well as of course, far more fully and richly beyond this life.

Jesus explained how the two realities can merge in our life here and now if we have faith: "But seek first his kingdom and his righteousness, and all these things [what we need in this life at the relative level] will be given to you as well" (Matthew 6:33).

Each of us needs to be vigilant to avoid the following outcome: "the worries of this life, the deceitfulness of wealth and the desires for other things come in and choke the word, making it unfruitful (Mark 4:19).

Money and possessions can be deceitful in providing a false sense of security. The truth is that money does not provide us with lasting security and happiness – no matter how much we have – either in this life, or in the life to come.

Research has shown that more money is not proportional to greater happiness. Many wealthy people still have led unhappy lives, and when they lost their money, such as in the Great Depression, some even committed suicide. Simply put, money does not provide authentic inner peace, genuine well-being, and lasting contentment – these are achieved only by seeking first the Kingdom of God.

Prayer and Spiritual Focus

When considering the importance of prayer, the following words can be instructive:

"Even people who do not think of themselves as religious, find to their amazement that when faced with death [or other calamity], whether their own or that of another, they suddenly not only want to call on some higher power, but actually start to do so, even without understanding what they mean by it. They might even start praying to go to a better place or another world where they will find help and guidance. ...

"I don't find it surprising that this kind of thing happens. In life we tend to think we can rely on our intellect and somehow keep control of our lives and our emotions. In the face of death [or a major setback], we suddenly feel the rug pulled out from beneath us. The rigid logic of our intellect is no use to us in this situation, and our usual ways of keeping control fall apart. We are torn apart, worse than naked, hanging there in shock and confusion, with nowhere to turn. This is when the intuitive sense that we are not alone kicks in, and we may find ourselves linking into an intuitive sense that there is more to life than we thought and we are going to have to rely on some other power, not just ourselves." (Hookham, Lama Shenpen. *There's More to Dying than Death.* Cambridge, UK: Windhorse Publications, 2012)

To realize that we need to rely on a Higher Power – not just ourselves – can apply equally when we have suffered loss as a result of having been unwittingly taken advantage of in a devious scam, or through fire, flood, or any number of other factors. In the broader context of life, we can never solve all our problems by ourselves alone (while of course, we have a responsibility to do our part.)

We can remind ourselves of the availability of help from Beyond – indeed, we are not alone. The universe consists of many worlds teeming with different kinds of benevolent beings.

In summary, we should never forget the importance and power of prayer. This entails remaining close to God and always seeking guidance. Another aspect is continued mindfulness and not falling into the trap of self-reliance and independence.

Faith in God

A painful scam loss, or another difficult situation, can precipitate a deeper evaluation of who we really are and why we are here.

Upon a heartfelt reflection on life, some begin to realize that human effort alone may not be adequate for their emotional, mental, or physical recovery and going on with life. They come to see that the advice of "get tough and try harder" is not a satisfactory answer. In fact, such admonition could by itself lead to burnout, further discouragement, and depression.

In sharing with trusted people the anguish of having been taken advantage of in a scam – and having done all one could as far as reporting the crime to law enforcement authorities – sometimes the well-meaning advice given is: "There is nothing more that you can do but pray."

Such advice reflects an intuited realization that our "self-power" is simply inadequate. What is needed is "Other-Power" or something greater than ourselves.

This Other-Power is referred to in various ways by those who have sought a higher purpose for their lives. Some expressions are Source, First Cause, Ultimate Reality, Allah, Yahweh, Brahman, Tao, and God. In this book, the word "God" will be used, signifying the Source of love, mercy, help and moral authority.

In the context of physical and emotional suffering as a result of a painful scam, our faith in God and divine help is far more important and precious than money. Our money, after all, may one day fail, or be lost – and certainly will be left behind when we pass from this earth.

By contrast, divine help will never perish – it will remain as an everlasting source of refuge. It is Other-Power that will ultimately free us from the ocean of this world's suffering.

The New Testament exhorts and encourages people dealing with heartaches and difficulties: "In all this you greatly rejoice, though now for a little while you may have had to suffer grief in all kinds of trials. These have come so that the proven genuineness of your faith – of greater worth than gold, which perishes even though refined by fire – may result in praise, glory and honour ..." (1 Peter 1:6-7).

In our own scam situation – with its monetary loss, which in looking back was merciful and not overwhelming – while we have become financially poorer, to more than compensate, we have become spiritually richer with renewed faith and spiritual growth.

Ultimately, faith in God and resulting prayer will help us in far more lasting ways than what money could ever achieve in our short lives on earth. In the meantime, a faith-filled life will also restore our joy of living.

Acceptance

After recognizing that we had been victims of a nasty financial scam, our minds were reeling with thoughts and feelings of disbelief, betrayal and misery, as well as asking, how on earth could we have been so deceived and acted in such irrational ways? Would life ever return to the well-being we had before the scam?

Befriending What Happened

Amidst our post-scam trauma, the following words were a good reminder about the realities of life: "Like waves in the ocean, all things are impermanent." The quote continues with a solution: "I will accept whatever happens and make it my friend." (Yongey Mingyur Rinpoche)

This life is fleeting. By *befriending* everything that occurs in our lives, we can use our experiences as opportunities for spiritual transformation.

In relation to our scam, we realized that to *fight* the situation (such as filing a lawsuit) was not the solution. This would only nurture annoyance, dislike, frustration, aversion, anger, hatred or aggression, as well as a measure of pride. Also, it would keep the flames of pain and hurt alive.

To engage in a *flight* response was likewise not the answer. It was escapism – withdrawing, avoiding, running away. Nothing would be achieved or resolved. Worse still, aversion, anger, hatred, and so forth, would continue.

To simply *freeze* was also not an option. This would be a form of denial of the whole situation, and leave us immobilised and paralysed as far as any constructive action.

Therefore, to "make it my *friend*" was indeed the way forward into healing. To befriend the situation and persons involved meant that we could learn from it all – to understand it, gain life-changing insights, and then live with humility and compassion.

Additionally, to befriend the situation meant putting into practice love and compassion – both for ourselves and the perpetrators. Instead of fighting or denying the situation, we could welcome it. Accepting what happened and the persons involved was indeed a form of love and compassion – opening the heart and mind instead of contracting and withdrawing into our own cocoons.

This then, we learnt, was how true *freedom* from pain and suffering would come after the scam.

After coming to acceptance, we were able to gradually let the situation go. Thoughts, memories, and feelings no longer triggered us as frequently. However, letting go was not simply giving up — we still needed to do all that we could to achieve healing and restore our wellbeing.

Unconditional Acceptance

The power of acceptance is in stopping to resist and finding the lesson in a situation.

"Of course, there is no formula for success except, perhaps, an unconditional acceptance of life and what it brings." (Arthur Rubinstein)

Part of the beauty and challenge of life is that it is unpredictable. Nothing is permanent, everything changes, and a lot of things can happen that will impact our life and transform who we are. To make the most of this reality, we need to cultivate the ability to truly accept whatever comes and embrace it. We need to develop the habit of looking at whatever happens through a positive mindset instead of a negative, defeatist one.

Of course, life will bring many challenges, such as losses, unexpected deaths of loved ones, terminal illness, etc., and it is not easy to embrace them when we are suffering and wishing those things would have never happened. But if we start cultivating acceptance in our lives now, we will likely cope with future crises in a different way and view them from a different perspective. We will be more likely to accept, instead of resisting.

We might want things to be different in the future, but in the present moment we need to accept things as they are. That is the way we can make our life flow smoothly instead of roughly. We will discover that we are happier and more peaceful when we accept what has happened instead of constantly fighting to change things.

Acceptance is a choice – a hard one, but a choice nonetheless. There are two ways out of a problem: accept what is happening, see the positive, and choose a peaceful state of mind; or fight against it, be miserable, and struggle against the universe.

Whether it is a family loss, a missed opportunity, or a sudden change in our plans, being able to accept things that are out of our control will help us maintain inner peace and happiness.

Acceptance can be a key to converting momentary happiness to ongoing happiness. It helps us move from feeling happy when things go well to actually being happy, no matter what is happening in our life.

Practicing acceptance prepares us to live in this changing world, where we never know what is going to happen next. Acceptance is like protecting ourself with our own shield.

Of course, we need to understand that acceptance is not related to weakness, and neither is it a synonym for conformity or mediocrity. We need to learn how to identify when it is time to persist and when it is time to accept.

Finally, finding the lesson or purpose behind every challenge will help us embrace it instead of fighting it.

(Based on https://tinybuddha.com/blog/the-power-of-acceptance-stop-resisting-and-find-the-lesson/)

A.C.C.E.P.T.

We once created an acronym with the letters A.C.C.E.P.T. The steps of this acronym apply to all people we deal with in life, including the scammers that had bitterly betrayed us.

Together and in an interconnected way, we are all in this mystery called life, with its joys and sorrows. Yet, receiving and accepting one another is not always easy. The acronym, A.C.C.E.P.T., can remind us of six sublime truths about living life.

Allowing – give people the freedom and joy to be themselves, and steer away from projecting unnecessary expectations, demands, and judgments on them.

Naturally, in the case of the scammers, their hurtful, non-virtuous behaviour could not be accepted – we always need to separate the "sin from the sinner". We ought to love all people, yet without tolerating or condoning unethical actions.

Cherishing – cherish people equal to our self-cherishing, and show them loving kindness whenever possible.

We realized that each scammer is a human being, who like us, wants to be happy and free from suffering. Yet, due to the law of causality, their actions will only further their suffering – for which we need compassion.

Compassion – care for people's welfare and well-being, deeply desiring to alleviate any suffering.

May each scammer realize that the pain and suffering they are inflicting on others will return to them in like manner due to the law of cause and effect. To avoid fully reaping what they have sown, may they come to deeply regret their deeds, and undertake positive remedial actions.

Equanimity – strive to be free of attachment and aversion, and show goodwill equally to all.

Even as we were unwittingly caught in a scam situation, we showed kindness and respect to the scammer who was dealing with us – and this we have not regretted. Because we were not filled with animosity toward the person even after we realized that we had been scammed, our prayer for them has been sincere and heartfelt.

Patience – endure challenging situations with people, and refrain from quickly reacting with anger or aggression. Realize that hatred breeds more hatred and is only conquered by love.

In looking back, we did not respond to the scammer with anger and hatred even after we realized it was a scam and clearly felt the hurt and pain. We have since patiently waited to see how the authorities may resolve our case.

Thankfulness – be grateful for our precious human existence, because any life can end quickly and unexpectedly. Extend empathetic joy toward others, rejoicing with them in their happiness and successes (why be envious and jealous?).

In relation to the scam, we are thankful for all that we have come to understand and for even being able to reach out to others with a book and a website, dedicated to helping them to journey through a scam or other kinds of loss and trauma.

These noble qualities of goodwill – when used with all-important discernment and wisdom – are an ideal way of relating to all living beings. They free the heart and mind from needless suffering and unhappiness – which has been the case with our own upsetting financial setback.

In summary, here are lessons we have learnt:

Accept all life's situations, remembering that we cannot change the past or guarantee the future. We can only live and act in the present.

Whatever life brings us, it is *as it is*. The Serenity Prayer is apropos in this context: "God grant me the serenity to accept the things I cannot change; courage to change the things I can; and wisdom to know the difference."

"If you know how to make good use of the mud, you can grow beautiful lotuses. If you know how to make good use of suffering, you can produce happiness. We need some suffering to make happiness possible." (Thich Nhat Hanh)

Trust that all things, indeed, can work together for good (Romans 8:28).

Focus on the Positive

"The power of positive thinking" is a well-known axiom made famous by Dale Carnegie. Many motivational speakers have referred to this maxim, and those who applied it have benefited from it.

How and what we choose to think determines how we feel and what we do. In the Old Testament book of Proverbs, this principle is stated as: "For as he thinks in his heart, so is he" (Prov. 23:7).

Henry Ford once aptly verbalized the importance of a positive attitude: "Whether you think you can or whether you think you can't, you're right!"

The following poem illustrates the importance of focusing on the positive:

Thinking

If you think you are beaten – you are.
If you think you dare not – you don't,
If you'd like to win, but think you can't
It's almost a cinch you won't.

If you think you'll lose – you've lost
For out in the world we find,
Success begins with a fellow's will
It's all in the state of mind.

Spiritual Lessons and Insights

If you think you're outclassed, you are
You've got to think high to rise,
You've got to be sure of yourself before
You can ever win a prize.

Life's battles don't always go
To the stronger or faster man,
But sooner or later the man who wins
Is the one who thinks he can!

Walter D. Wintle (written in the late 19th or early 20th century)

After suffering the anguish of having been scammed, a positive attitude will be important in recovery.

In the end, we are responsible for our own destiny – achieved first through developing a positive attitude, then taking needed action to deal with our challenges, and making changes to improve our lives. Simply running from difficulties and quitting is never the solution to fulfilling our potential and realizing our dreams and goals.

Overcoming the hopelessness, helplessness, and depression following a serious scam is not easy. However, if we can adopt a positive attitude, we may be pleasantly surprised what we can do. And, the scam will not remain as a painful memory, but a springboard to greater success and fulfillment in life.

A positive attitude and view will keep us from two pitfalls in dealing with a scam or another misfortune.

These snares are: first, desperately trying to change the depressing situation; or second, letting the experience determine who we are.

Rather, a positive outlook will help us realize that trials and challenges are an inevitable part of life. It will also help us persevere through those hardships.

Tara Brach notes: "Seeing goodness does not mean we ignore problems or deny difficulties. It's not about wearing rose-colored glasses. It's about evolving past some of that negativity bias so that we can genuinely see what's good and nourish it in ourselves and others.

"Seeing goodness is seeing with the eyes of wisdom and a kind heart, much as a caring grandfather or grandmother might."

Recognize and appreciate the mercy shown in the trial. Whatever happens to us, it could always be worse. Try to see the silver lining on the dark cloud.

For example, in situations of widespread bushfires, in some cases, only the outer sheds on a property may have been destroyed, while the house was protected. Another case of mercy could be a theft where the victim is not financially hurting, but still able to meet their day-to-day expenses.

The Old Testament story of Job is instructive. While Job suffered grievously through multiple losses, later what he lost was more than restored, and he learned precious lessons in addition. "After Job had prayed for his friends, the Lord restored his fortunes and gave him twice as much as he had before." (Job 42:10) Is there a yet physically unseen chance of restoring the loss that is worth hoping for?

Here is a timeless advice for fostering a positive attitude in our lives: "Finally, brothers and sisters, whatever is true, whatever is noble, whatever is right, whatever is pure, whatever is lovely, whatever is admirable—if anything is excellent or praiseworthy—think about such things" (Philippians 4:8).

Gratitude

When we realize that we have been victims of a scam and suffered a painful loss, gratitude will be the furthest thing from our minds. Instead, there will be denial ("this simply can't be true"), anger ("why has this happened to me?"), bargaining ("maybe I can yet change it") and depression ("I feel very sad and lonely in all this"). This is the grieving process.

Allow the grieving to occur – the real feelings and emotions cannot just be denied, attempted to be ignored, or willed away. Rather, to mourn a loss is natural, normal and healthy.

Yet, in processing the situation, we can also look for positive aspects to be grateful for. What good has emerged from the bitter situation? We may also see how we were spared from a worse scenario.

A thankful heart and counting our blessings are very powerful in reorienting one's perspective and transcending sadness and despair. Research studies have shown the benefits of gratitude including less anxiety and depression, sounder sleep, better health, higher long-term satisfaction with life, and kinder behaviour toward others.

Buddhist teacher, Yongey Mingyur Rinpoche, has written, "Seeing its many wonderful qualities, I rejoice and delight in this human life." This statement epitomizes gratitude and appreciation for whatever happens in life.

Tara Brach, meditation teacher, psychologist and author, has written that "in addition to the ways we serve, it's by savouring moments, feeling the sweetness of gratitude that we arrive most fully in our lives. As philosopher, Meister Eckhart, put it, 'If the only prayer you said in your whole life was, 'Thank you,' it would suffice.'"

In the aftermath of the recent tragic flooding in parts of Australia, families who had lost almost everything have commented to television reporters: "At least we have each other; our pets are safe; and we still have a roof over our head. So many people, including strangers, have come to our aid."

For some, thankfulness may arise in realizing such blessings as:

Good health – no major illness, accident, injuries or disabilities.

Few major losses – for example, no break-ins into the home, car theft, ID theft, or other theft of major significance.

No weather or fire damage to anything.

Having money to cover all needs and savings for emergency.

Happy marriage and family.

Purpose and meaning in life.

In addition to gratitude, we need to consider what many others have faced – and practice heartfelt compassion. Some of the tragic situations and circumstances people are presently experiencing include:

Serious illness and need for surgeries to get relief from pain.

Poverty, inability to pay rent or find a place to rent, resulting in homelessness.

Loss of life savings or retirement funds through a devastating scam operation or a financial institution collapse.

Break-ins and theft, vandalism, property damage.

Physical injury – including personal attacks, assaults, and sexual molestation.

Loss of a family member through medical malpractice, drunk driving, violent crime, or suicide.

Major losses through flood, fire, or another destructive event.

In conclusion, the apostle Paul urges: "Do not get drunk on wine, which leads to debauchery. Instead, be filled with the Spirit ... always giving thanks to God the Father for everything, in the name of our Lord Jesus Christ (Ephesians 5:18, 20).

Preciousness Time

This human existence is invaluable because it provides the opportunity to not only pursue material goals, but more importantly, to cultivate our spiritual development.

At the end of our earthly life, the body will die and over time, disintegrate into its constituent elements. However, our consciousness (others may use terms such as, mind, awareness, spirit or soul), will continue in another realm — together with the karma we have generated. Our status in the next life will be based on our virtuous or non-virtuous actions in this life. The universal cosmic law of cause and effect — or the law of compensation — will continue acting, and even more reliably so than here on earth. Based on their previous actions, some will experience great happiness, while others will, for a time, go through painful suffering.

In this life, therefore, we have the opportunity to accomplish something meaningful, rather than just spending our time and energy pursuing the passing pleasures of life.

To have this precious time and not use it wisely represents a lack of wisdom and great loss. Rather, we should use this gift of life and time to develop our potential and thereby bring benefit and happiness to countless living beings.

We should reflect deeply on the preciousness of time. Ponder with compassion those who spend their time and energy on trivial worldly pursuits, or are destroying their opportunity for spiritual development by harming others.

Allow your contemplation to inspire within you the compassionate wish to wisely use your time for the greatest benefit of all living beings — both now and in the future.

(Based on *Heart of Dharma Collection*, found at https://sourcepointglobaloutreach.org/)

In relation to the preciousness of time, we must contemplate the fact that death is inevitable. At some point, death will come to each of us. It is the natural outgrowth of impermanence. With each passing moment we are closer to our death, which will come regardless of whether or not we have made time to pursue higher values and a spiritual path.

While death is certain, the time of our death is uncertain — we do not know when death will occur. Each day we encounter numerous dangers that could cause our demise. At the time of death, our wealth, possessions, and even cherished friends will not be able to help us. Money cannot buy us more time, happiness or peace. Friends can offer their love and support, but they cannot stop or delay death once our time is up.

Our body, when no longer able to support us, will be of no help at the time of death. Only the wisdom and our inner spiritual wealth that we have developed by pursuing higher values will remain with us.

By understanding impermanence and death, we realize the preciousness of time and can choose to embrace what is truly of value. We will wisely discern how we spend our valuable time and energy, and will make a determined effort to live an ethical lifestyle, cultivate virtue, and serve the welfare of all living beings.

(Based on *Heart of Dharma Collection* found at https://sourcepointglobaloutreach.org/)

In summary, we must remain conscious of the preciousness of time and make the best use of it. For seniors, such as ourselves, this is even more critical, because we simply do not have many years left. Soberly, it could be fewer than we think, because the end of life can come unexpectedly and quickly.

Our experience of the distressing financial scam reinforced our need to be continually aware of the preciousness of time. As a result, we formulated three aspirations, in the form of three questions, to always bear in mind and ask often:

– Is this the best use of my/our precious time?
– Is this task/activity necessary or needed to be done?
– Am I wasting my precious time on what is trivia and an unprofitable pursuit?

These three questions are useful when receiving door salespeople, marketing phone calls, unsolicited emails, and stands in shopping malls. One must politely, yet firmly, resist having one's precious time swallowed up by marketers and the ensuing conversations. This advice would have served us well when we were first addressed by the scammer over the phone – but it is never too late to learn (even if it is through the school of hard knocks)!

Finally, the New Testament admonishes us to guard our precious time and use it in the best way:

"Be very careful, then, how you live — not as unwise but as wise, making the most of every opportunity, because the days are evil. Therefore do not be foolish, but understand what the Lord's will is. Do not get drunk on wine, which leads to debauchery. Instead, be filled with the Spirit." (Ephesians 5:15-18)

"Be wise in the way you act ... make the most of every opportunity." (Colossians 4:5)

"Who is wise and understanding among you? Let him show it by his good life, by deeds done in the humility that comes from wisdom. But if you harbor bitter envy and selfish ambition in your hearts, do not boast about it or deny the truth. Such 'wisdom' does not come down from heaven but is earthly, unspiritual, of the devil. For where you have envy and selfish ambition, there you find disorder and every evil practice.

"But the wisdom that comes from heaven is first of all pure; then peace-loving, considerate, submissive, full of mercy and good fruit, impartial and sincere. Peacemakers who sow in peace raise a harvest of righteousness." (James 3:13-18)

Eight Worldly Concerns

Experiencing a painful financial scam reminded us of the wisdom of a Buddhist teaching about the "eight worldly concerns."

The eight worldly concerns classify the attachments and aversions that yoke us to life in this world and the cycle of suffering. They are four hopes and corresponding four fears, which we cycle through endlessly – or until we discover an authentic spiritual path which will include freeing us from these concerns.

The eight worldly concerns (or preoccupations) cycle of hope and fear tends to dominate our lives from day to day and moment to moment: hope for happiness and fear of suffering; hope for fame and fear of insignificance; hope for praise and fear of blame; and hope for gain and fear of loss. We spend our lives trying to hold onto some things and get rid of others in an endless and stressful struggle.

You could ask, what is wrong with preferring happiness to sadness or praise to blame? Isn't the pursuit of happiness what it is all about? Isn't it obvious that gain is better than loss?

There is nothing wrong with these as such, but it is one thing to recognize what we would like to attract and what we would prefer to get rid of, and quite another to be obsessed with getting our way and terrified of things going wrong.

The problem is that hope is joined at the hip with its partner, fear. We can't have one without the other. When we are caught in this hope-fear cycle, our attitude is always tense and even our most satisfying experiences are bounded by paranoia.

In the first set of hope and fear, we look at things in terms of happiness versus suffering, pleasure versus pain. We hope for happiness, but once we have it, fear arises, for we are afraid to lose it. Out of that fear we cling to pleasure so hard that the pleasure itself becomes a form of pain. And when suffering arises, no amount of wishful thinking makes it go away. The more we hope for it to be otherwise, the more pain we feel.

In the second set of hope and fear, we can be obsessed with fame and afraid of our own insignificance. We scramble our way to the top, hungry for confirmation, and when it is not forthcoming, we get turned off and huffy. Then when it dawns on us how hard we need to work to be seen as someone special, our fear of insignificance is magnified. Behind our façade of fame, we suffer from a kind of inner desolation and hollowness.

With the third set, we become obsessed with praise and fearful of blame. We need to be pumped up constantly or we begin to have doubts about our worth. When we are not searching for praise, we are busy trying to cover up our mistakes so we don't get caught. But there is never enough praise to satisfy us, and we are never free from the threat of being found wanting. Only if we are perfect can we count on continual praise, but although we struggle for perfection, we can never attain it. The slightest little mistake is all it takes to retrigger our fear.

With the fourth set, we are obsessed with gain and loss. We invest in situations with high hopes, and expect things to continue improving. That quality of hope is so seductive that we forget how easily situations can turn on us. Just as we are about to congratulate ourselves on our success, the bottom falls out, and fear once again holds sway. Our hope falls apart and we are afraid that things will keep going downhill forever. Over and over, things are hopeful one moment and discouraging the next, and in either case we are anxious.

These cycles of hope and fear can occupy our minds and capture our energy. No matter what is happening to us, we think it could be better, or at least different. No matter who we are, we think we could be better, or at least different. Nothing is ever good enough and we can never relax.

Spiritual Lessons and Insights

(Based on Lief, Judy. "The Middle Way of Stress". Lion's Roar Magazine. See https://www.lionsroar.com/the-middle-way-of-stress-september-2012/)

In summary, we need to catch ourselves when being preoccupied with the "eight worldly concerns". They can unwittingly become obsessions where our actions are governed by attachment and aversion:
– hope for happiness and fear of suffering
– hope for fame and fear of insignificance
– hope for praise and fear of blame
– hope for gain and fear of loss

How true to life these eight worldly pre-occupations can be! In relation to our loss, we were happy while our finances were secure and being added to through our pensions and interest. Our spirits plummeted after the scam – the loss experienced and the way it happened.

We realized that changing external events, many of which are inconsequential in the long-run – should not make our feelings continually go up and down like a yo-yo – sometimes several times in a day! Of course, this is not to negate the seriousness of the crime we had fallen victims to – and for which responsible action had to be taken, such as informing the bank and police.

In time, we finally reached a level of acceptance and equanimity where we recognized that gain and loss are a natural part of life – we "win some and lose some" as a dear older friend once shared with us.

Love of Money

One of the immediate lessons of loss through a financial scam is how attached we can become to our money. The money itself may not be the problem – rather it is the strong feelings of attachment that cause the grief and misery over the loss.

A financial loss can also remind us of impermanence, which is an inherent quality of all things physical. Recognizing this fact can bring us to considering what happens after we die, which in turn can reduce our clinging to material possessions – including money.

Even those who are extremely rich in this life will, once they die, leave everything behind. We cannot take even one penny with us. If we have great stores of food, we cannot take any of it. All our friends and relatives will stay behind once it is our time to depart this world. We will not even take our physical body with us.

The only thing that survives death is our soul and consciousness. Whether we were rich or poor, famous or unknown, beautiful or ugly, none of it will make any difference when we die. The only thing that will help us at the time is whatever character and soul development we were able to achieve during our lifetime. If we can be confident in that, we can die at peace and have no fear.

In summary, we ought not to become overly attached to, or in love with, our money – or with any of the physical possessions that we may accrue through our wealth, such as homes, cars, boats, and other creature comforts. Our attachment to these physical things needs to be severed, so that we do not lose sight of higher values.

While money is important to live on and cover our expenses, the pursuit of more and more wealth can unwittingly become an idol, and spiritually unprofitable, futile, and even damaging. Studies have shown that after a point, more money will not bring increasing or lasting or happiness.

The Bible gives earnest admonition to not fall prey to the love of money – and so not suffer misery when some of it is lost. These three passages are rich in meaning:

"Cast but a glance at riches, and they are gone, for they will surely sprout wings and fly off to the sky like an eagle." (Proverbs 23:5)

"But godliness with contentment is great gain. For we brought nothing into the world, and we can take nothing out of it. But if we have food and clothing, we will be content with that. People who want to get rich fall into temptation and a trap and into many foolish and harmful desires that plunge men into ruin and destruction. For the love of money is a root of all kinds of evil. Some people, eager for money, have wandered from the faith and pierced themselves with many griefs." (1 Timothy 6:6-10)

"Keep your lives free from the love of money and be content with what you have, because God has said, 'Never will I leave you; never will I forsake you.' So we say with confidence, 'The Lord is my helper; I will not be afraid. What can man do to me?'" (Heb. 13:5-6)

Generosity

Generosity is the enlightened quality of giving and charity. Its essence is unconditional love – a boundless openness of heart and mind, selfless giving which is completely free from attachment and expectation in the form of any selfish desire for gratitude, recognition, advantage, reputation, or any other worldly reward. From the depths of our heart, we generously offer our love, compassion, time, energy, and resources to serve the highest welfare of all beings.

The true essence of generosity is not in just the action of giving, or the value of the gift. Rather, it is in our motivation of genuine concern for others – the generous motivation of the awakened heart of compassion, wisdom and love.

In addition, our practice of giving should be free of discrimination regarding who is worthy and who is unworthy to receive.

To cultivate generosity, it is wise to contemplate the benefits of this practice, the disadvantages of being miserly, as well as the fact that our body and our wealth are impermanent. With this in mind, we will be encouraged to use both our body and wealth to practice generosity while we can.

Generosity is a cure for the afflictions of greed, miserliness and possessiveness. In the practice of giving, we may offer our time, energy, money, food, clothing, or gifts to assist others.

We may also offer the priceless treasure of authentic spiritual instruction, sharing wisdom and spiritual principles. This offering can free others from misperceptions that cause confusion, pain and suffering.

Giving includes delivering living beings (insects, animals and people) from harm, distress, fear and terror. In this way, we offer care and comfort, helping others to feel safe and peaceful. We do this selflessly, though wisdom and discernment would be needed in any risky situation.

We practice generosity in an especially powerful way when we continually embrace all living beings in the radiant love of our heart.

(Based on http://sourcepointglobaloutreach.org/what-we-offer/ The *Heart of Dharma Collection*)

Experiencing a financial scam made us reflect on our own generosity. Had we become too isolated and sheltered in our retirement years – as well as unconcerned, and even miserly, toward others? We renewed our determination to practice generosity as we are able to. The following quotes spoke to us:

"The mindfulness and compassion that helps you be present for yourself also helps you connect more fully with others. When you feel connected to someone, your concern and generosity grows. Not as an onerous responsibility, or because you're supposed to be generous, but because with growing mindfulness and compassion, you feel a natural relatedness. You are sensitive to their happiness and struggles, and it's natural to help." (Tara Brach and Jack Kornfield)

"Generosity is not about saintly behaviour, but simple human caring. Our way of being generous and serving doesn't mean just giving money, but offering time, concern, help, sympathetic support. The most successful manager in a software company and the aid cleaning hospital rooms with a spirit of good cheer both spread wellbeing wherever they go. A growing body of research points to something we each intuitively understand. Generosity goes hand in hand with happiness. In acts of giving, parts of the brain associated with happiness light up. Spending money on others makes us happier than spending it on ourselves." (Tara Brach and Jack Kornfield)

Finally, the New Testament encourages each of us to be generous – with promises of blessings. The first passage is an especially amazing example of faith, devotion and generosity.

"Jesus sat down opposite the place where the offerings were put and watched the crowd putting their money into the temple treasury. Many rich people threw in large amounts. But a poor widow came and put in two very small copper coins, worth only a fraction of a penny.

"Calling his disciples to him, Jesus said, 'I tell you the truth, this poor widow has put more into the treasury than all the others. They all gave out of their wealth; but she, out of her poverty, put in everything – all she had to live on.'" (Mark 12:41-44)

"Remember this: Whoever sows sparingly will also reap sparingly, and whoever sows generously will also reap generously. Each man should give what he has decided in his heart to give, not reluctantly or under compulsion, for God loves a cheerful giver. And God is able to make all grace abound to you, so that in all things at all times, having all that you need, you will abound in every good work.

"As it is written: 'He has scattered abroad his gifts to the poor; his righteousness endures forever.' Now he who supplies seed to the sower and bread for food will also supply and increase your store of seed and will enlarge the harvest of your righteousness. You will be made rich in every way so that you can be generous on every occasion, and through us your generosity will result in thanksgiving to God. This service that you perform is not only supplying the needs of God's people but is also overflowing in many expressions of thanks to God." (2 Corinthians 9:6–12)

"In everything I did, I showed you that by this kind of hard work we must help the weak, remembering the words the Lord Jesus himself said: 'It is more blessed to give than to receive.'" (Acts 20:35)

Cause and Effect (Karma)

Everyone is familiar with the universal law of cause and effect, also referred to as the law of karma or the law of compensation. The Bible is unequivocal in that respect:

"Sow for yourselves righteousness, reap the fruit of unfailing love, and break up your unplowed ground; for it is time to seek the LORD, until he comes and showers righteousness on you." (Hosea 10:12)

"As I have observed, those who plow evil and those who sow trouble reap it." (Job 4:8)

"The wicked man earns deceptive wages, but he who sows righteousness reaps a sure reward." (Proverbs 11:18)

"He who sows wickedness reaps trouble, and the rod of his fury will be destroyed." (Proverbs 22:8)

Karma is indeed real (yet a complex matter for us to fully understand as mortals). It may in part account for bad things happening to ourselves or others, or for different outcomes in difficult situations.

For example, why do some encounter an agonizing loss where their life savings disappear at the hands of merciless scammers or a failed money institution, and others, while their loss is traumatic, only lose a relatively small portion of their savings? Or, in bushfire situations, why are some homes burnt to the ground and others spared when the wind direction suddenly changes?

The law of karma posits that there is no suffering without a prior cause. Sometimes the correlation between cause and effect is crystal clear. At other times, however, tracing the cause for someone's or our own suffering can be very difficult. This is because the reason for our suffering may or may not be with ourselves or our actions. In this life, the law of karma is not clear-cut, but rather complex.

To be sure that our past or recent actions are not the karmic cause of our present misfortune and suffering, it is good to thoroughly assess our lives in terms of thoughts, intents, motives, and resulting actions. To regularly survey the circumstances of our life to discern the karmic patterns established in the past is a beneficial spiritual practice.

We can also check our current thoughts and actions as an indication of what will in time come. Others may praise us for our fine behaviour, but only we truly know if our actions are tainted with impure motivation or poisonous emotions.

No person prefers suffering to happiness, yet sadly, almost all of us create causes for misery. This is because we often act oblivious to karmic consequences, seeking gratification in the moment. We then blame our bad fortune, which could be a direct result of our own conduct, on negative outer circumstances.

It is however possible that a given negative event in our lives was not the result of our own sin, but we were simply in the wrong place at the wrong time and affected by the sin/s of others.

Sooner or later, our souls must journey on beyond this life into other realms – stripped of everything except our soul, consciousness, and the forces of karma. Some may seemingly get away with not paying the penalties for committed wrongs in this life. However, the law of compensation works far more exactly and reliably in the next life, and all who engaged in evil, dishonest or unethical actions will certainly bear the results of their actions then.

In being aware of the law of compensation, and in the context of being taken advantage of by scammers, we can use the situation to arouse compassion. We can imagine the karmic forces that will overtake cruel scammers after they die – unless they turn from their evil ways. And, proportionate misfortune may well catch up with them in this life. The comfortable lives of some scammers could suddenly be changed by tragedy – the unexpected consequence of their unsuspected karma!

Rather than continuing to act in ignorance with respect to karma, we each need to refine our sense of what to accept and what to reject and continually work on purifying our lives. Rather than quickly blaming others when things go wrong, consider the possibility of your actions having contributed to the problem.

We can endeavour to – through well-disciplined actions, well-chosen words, and beneficial intentions – create the causes for fortunate circumstances. Ultimately, of course, may we all escape the bewildering tangle of karma altogether and fully enter the state of the divine realm.

(Based on Tromge, Jane. *Ngondro Commentary*. Junction City, CA: Padma Publishing, 1995.)

In summary, we need to remain aware of the reality of karma (the law of cause and effect or law of compensation). "When causes and conditions come together, a result is sure to follow. So I will do my best to help others and engage in positive deeds." (Yongey Mingyur Rinpoche)

Whatever we sow, we shall, in due time, also reap – both good or bad outcomes. The reaping may not occur immediately, or in this life, but it will come, even in our next realm of existence. May we maintain this awareness in all our thoughts and actions.

When things go wrong, we need to examine our lives for non-virtuous actions that may have brought this about. While all trials are not the result of our own non-virtuous actions, self-examination is a good spiritual practice – being instructive and growth-producing.

If we recognize that we have acted unwisely and unethically, and earnestly change our ways, with remorse and positive remedial action, then the bad effects of karma may be lessened.

Here is a concluding Bible passage: "Do not be deceived: God cannot be mocked. A man reaps what he sows. The one who sows to please his sinful nature, from that nature will reap destruction; the one who sows to please the Spirit, from the Spirit will reap eternal life." (Galatians 6:7-8)

Mindfulness

One of the most important lessons we learnt from our financial scam was that of mindfulness. As the events of that fateful day unfolded, we should have been far more mindful of our feelings and thoughts – as well as the manipulation we succumbed to with the resulting loss.

Mindfulness is a present-centred, non-judging awareness. Decades of science and clinical research have shown that mindfulness practices can dramatically and positively impact our physical health, emotional resilience, mental clarity, and enjoyment of life. (Tara Brach)

The first step in mindfulness is pausing to become present. We live in a stressful time. Many of us are facing the demands of life at the fast pace of our culture. As a result, we can easily lose connection with ourselves and with what matters most.

Mindfulness is paying attention to what is happening inside and outside of us in the present moment. This begins with something very simple – a pause. Imagine being in a movie theatre immersed in a fast-paced thriller. Suddenly, the screen freezes. No longer swept away in the action, you become aware of where you are, the people around you, the pulsing tension in your body, your thoughts and feelings. You are in a pause.

Learning to pause in the midst of your life brings you back to what is actually happening. You are not caught up in the movie, and in that space of a pause, you can see more clearly what you are thinking and feeling and what is going on around you.

With mindfulness, it is possible to pause, breathe, and find a space of more clarity and empathy. You can then remember what is really important and respond in a wise, kind, and balanced way. The pause frees you from repeating old patterns that no longer serve you. (Jack Kornfield)

(Based on Tara Brach and Jack Kornfield. "The 40-Day Mindfulness Daily Program".)

The times we are most caught in reactivity is when we are least inclined to call on mindfulness. Yet, without mindfulness, we run the risk of reacting and creating more conflict, misunderstanding and harm.

The following is a mindfulness tool that offers help for working with difficult emotions in any situation. With an acronym, R.A.I.N., it directs our attention in a clear and systematic way that helps cut through confusion and stress. The four steps are:

R – Recognize what is happening.
A – Allow life to be just as it is.
I – Investigate with a gentle attention.
N – Nurture with kindness.

Recognize What Is Happening

"Recognize" means noticing whatever thoughts, emotions, or sensations are arising right here and now. Often, the question, "What is happening inside me right now?" helps focus our attention in an immediate way.

Allow Life to Be Just as It Is

"Allowing" is letting be the thoughts, emotions or sensations we discover, so even when the last thing we want is to feel the rawness of fear or helplessness, just having the intention to allow or let be helps us to pause and be present. For some, mentally whispering a phrase, such as "yes" or "this too" deepens the pause. These words encourage us to give space to what is going on, so this constitutes the allowing.

Investigate with a Gentle Attention

"Investigate with gentleness" means that when an emotion is strong, we deepen our mindfulness by bringing a curious, respectful attention to what is happening. Investigating is not a mental activity. We are not analysing why we are behaving in a certain way. Rather, investigating means inquiring, asking where the feelings are in our body and directly contacting the felt sense of our experience. While it may help us discover a limiting belief, investigating primarily focuses on where we currently feel stuck or vulnerable, and what that part of us needs the most.

Nurture with Kindness

"Nurture with kindness" allows us to respond to what the vulnerable or stuck part of ourselves needs. Often, the unmet need is for acceptance, care, compassion, forgiveness or understanding. Inwardly offering care by sending a message of kindness and understanding allows us to reconnect with our resourcefulness and move on.

Just as after a rain, the natural world blossoms, the same occurs after you do the steps of R.A.I.N. There is an inner opening – a healing, a realization. When you have completed the steps, it is essential to pause and simply rest in what you are experiencing. When R.A.I.N. is done fully, the story of self can be washed away, leaving a sense of aliveness, immediacy, creativity and freedom. Even when R.A.I.N. is incomplete, you will still notice a shift with less of a sense of a stuck self.

R.A.I.N. is a useful strategy for slowing down and systematically bringing mindfulness and kindness to difficult emotions. You can do this on the spot in response to a challenging situation, or you can practice R.A.I.N. as applied mindfulness during a meditation.

As you allow yourself to receive this kind presence, you might then simply rest in the aftermath of R.A.I.N., the freedom of not being identified with the emotional pain. You're resting in your natural, compassionate awareness, in the sense of open-heartedness and presence, knowing that this awareness as the innermost truth of what you are.

(Based on Tara Brach and Jack Kornfield. Mindfulness Daily Program: "Resilience, Healing and Inner Freedom — Emotional Healing – Day 24)

In summary, and in relation to our financial scam experience, we have learnt to be especially mindful of our thoughts – which can lead to positive or negative feelings and actions.

A negative situation can change simply by mindfully changing our perspective about it. "The suffering of beings is mainly produced by the mind. I must free myself from my self-created bonds." (Yongey Mingyur Rinpoche)

We need to be mindfully aware of any faulty perception of a situation, which may lead us astray and cause suffering.

Below is a selection of quotations on the importance of our thoughts and mindfulness.

"Positive thoughts are more powerful than negative ones and you can choose which you pay attention to." (Paul Foreman, www.mindmapinspiration.com)

"Life is the movie you see through your own, unique eyes. It makes little difference what is happening out there. It's how you take it that counts." (Denis Waitley, *The Winner's Edge*)

"We are what we think. All that we are arises with our thoughts. With our thoughts we make the world. Speak or act with a pure mind and happiness will follow you as your shadow, unshakeable." (*The Dhammapada*)

"A loving person lives in a loving world. A hostile person lives in a hostile world. Everyone you meet is your mirror." (Ken Keyes, Jr., *Handbook to Higher Consciousness*)

"Life has a bright side and a dark side, for the world of relativity is composed of light and shadows. If you permit your thoughts to dwell on evil, you yourself will become ugly. Look only for the good in everything, that you absorb the quality of beauty." (Paramahansa Yogananda, *Sayings of Paramahansa Yogananda*)

"The world is a reflection of your thoughts. Change your thoughts, change your life." (Notsalmon.com)

May we all daily remain mindful and thereby live meaningful and virtuous lives, and not fall prey to unwholesome and non-virtuous behaviour. Amen.

Compassion

As we develop the mind of compassion, from the depths of our heart, we radiate in all directions the sincere wish for all living beings to be free from suffering and the causes of suffering. The immeasurable quality of compassion (or mercy) is a wise heartfelt motivation to relieve the pain, sorrow, and suffering of others.

Compassion arises from our genuine concern for others and manifests as selfless acts of physical and spiritual charity. With true compassion we have deep insight into the causes of human suffering. Therefore, we are able to serve others in wise, loving, calm, and skilful ways without being overwhelmed by feelings of pity, grief or sadness.

In this way, compassion opens the heart and dissolves cruelty, selfishness and narrowmindedness. Our compassion – the sincere wish that all beings be free from suffering – must extend beyond those to whom we feel close. It should embrace all living beings throughout all realms of existence for it to become sublime, limitless and immeasurable.

(Based on http://sourcepointglobaloutreach.org/what-we-offer/, The Heart of Dharma Collection)

Compassion is inherent in our nature as human beings. It is natural to us – we do not need to create it. Cultivating compassion does not mean injecting some new, improved element into ourselves so that we can work more effectively. Instead, we simply uncover the compassion that is already there. How do we begin? We start by examining the ways in which we mask this fundamental human quality.

Compassion has three components: awareness, friendliness, and openness.

We begin with awareness because it is important to be clear who we are – not who we wish to be, hope we are, and what others have told us we are or should be. When we are not constantly struggling to be something or somebody, we are not so hampered by our preconceptions, and can see more clearly.

Friendliness is an extension of awareness because, as we become more honest with ourselves and more willing to drop false identities, we feel a fresh sense of appreciation for who we are. It is a relief when we have nothing left to hide and nothing to promote. The warmth and appreciation that we feel when we begin to accept ourselves in turn leads to an increased appreciation of others.

By cultivating awareness and friendliness, we also begin to develop greater openness. As a result of greater awareness, experiences and identities that we took to be solid begin to crumble. We are less caught in fixed views and more open to new perspectives. As a result of greater friendliness, we begin to be more appreciative of ourselves and others. Not only are our views less solid, but our heart also begins to open up.

By cultivating awareness, friendliness and openness, we are making room for compassion to peek through. We discover that if there is an opening for it, compassion is always present. It arises on its own if we let it. It does not need to be forced but arises as a natural and appropriate response to the need at hand.

Compassion is based on empathy – being touched by the suffering of others. There are many levels of empathy. Someone who is greatly compassionate is so touched by the suffering of others that it cuts him deeply. He feels its sharpness as if it were a hair brushing the surface of his eye. Most of us are not that sensitive. When we notice the suffering of others, it is more like a hair brushing the palm of our hand.

Often, our sensitivity to suffering is limited. On top of that, we have learned to harden our hearts further as a way of coping with the intensity of life and death.

However, it is possible to reverse this closing-down process and reconnect with our heart. Instead of hiding from suffering, we could let ourselves feel its sharpness. Then our awareness, friendliness and openness can blossom into true compassion, which is the will and commitment to help all beings and to relieve suffering whenever we encounter it.

(Based on Shambhala Publications Authors. *Radical Compassion*. Boston, MA: Shambhala Publications, 2014.)

In summary, we need to cultivate and practice compassion for both the present and future suffering of people near and far – who are, or will be, reaping what either they themselves or others have sown.

Since all humans and the earth are interconnected, the effects of our virtuous and non-virtuous actions also interconnect and affect both ourselves and others.

In the context of the suffering brought about by scams, our compassionate hearts should especially extend to:

– Other victims of scam theft and loss – the numbers of whom are increasing – among which some may have been financially devastated and are grievously suffering.

– Perpetrators of scam and fraud who, while they may be presently living scot-free, will reap suffering and misery in their lives in due time. This, of course, is due to the unfailing universal law of cause and effect (the law of compensation) – which will continue to operate in their next life, based on their actions in this life. With our compassionate hearts, we may pray that those involved in perpetrating scams (and other crimes) will quickly awaken and recognize how their actions have brought untold misery and grief to others. May they then turn from their ways, before having to reap great suffering in their own lives!

Finally, may our compassion also embrace those who have lost homes, savings, family members, health, and other precious possessions through ways such as crime, malpractices, war, persecution, genocide, famine, disease, earthquakes, and weather disasters.

Forgiveness

When wronged – especially grievously or unjustly wronged – forgiveness can be very challenging. This is certainly true after having been cunningly taken advantage of in a scam. The feelings of betrayal, broken trust, and helplessness in dealing with the loss, as well as the recurring painful memories that are unexpectedly triggered, can make forgiveness extremely difficult.

Yet, forgiveness is still necessary – in fact, vital for our longer-term health and well-being. For example, it has been shown that repressed emotions – which would include emotions associated with unforgiveness – can contribute to chronic stress, which in turn could stimulate the production of cancer cells.

Forgiveness frees us from the power of the perpetrator, whereas unforgiveness and grudges keep us tied to the situation and in a victim mode. It has been wisely said that unforgiveness – and an associated root of bitterness – is like drinking poison and expecting the other person to die.

Additionally, forgiveness needs to be applied to both the perpetrator/s and ourselves. For example, with deep resentment, we build our case against the scammer. "The word *resentment* means 'to feel again'. Each time we repeat to ourselves a story of how we have been wronged, we feel again in our body and mind the anger at being violated. But often enough our resentment of others reflects our resentment of ourselves." (Brach, Tara. *Radical Acceptance*. New York: Bantam Books, 2003.)

At times, "you may find the unfinished business of the heart arising. The pains you carry from the past may appear, including those situations you've not been able to forgive. ... Forgiveness is the release of anger and blame to start anew. Without forgiveness, we remain chained to the past." (Tara Brach and Jack Kornfield)

In the context of forgiveness, the following verses from an ancient Buddhist text have much relevance:

1. Our life is shaped by our mind; we become what we think. Suffering follows an evil thought as the wheels of a cart follow the oxen that draw it.

2. Our life is shaped by our mind; we become what we think. Joy follows a pure thought like a shadow that never leaves.

3. "He was angry with me, he attacked me, he defeated me, he robbed me" – those who dwell on such thoughts will never be free from hatred.

4. "He was angry with me, he attacked me, he defeated me, he robbed me" – those who do not dwell on such thoughts will surely become free from hatred.

5. For hatred can never put an end to hatred; love alone can. This is an unalterable law.

6. People forget that their lives will end soon. For those who remember, quarrels come to an end. (Easwaran, Eknath. *The Dhammapada* (Easwaran's Classics of Indian Spirituality). Tomales, CA: Nilgiri Press, 2007)

From our hurtful scam experience, we have learnt that it was better not to dwell on the unfortunate and unpleasant experience – if at all possible. Otherwise, we were just perpetuating our pain and hurt – and unwittingly nurturing unforgiveness.

At the heart of forgiveness lies a precious understanding of our basic nature – that is, at the core of each human being is an ever-present goodness and love. The Hebrew Scriptures attest to this with the words, "God saw all that he had made, and it was very good" (Genesis 1:31).

Of course, over time and from our ancestors, our basic nature has become defiled, and we find anger, attachment, jealousy and pride, among many other undesirable traits. However, our underlying basic goodness is never obliterated and can again be restored. Recognizing our basic human goodness is a gateway to a forgiving and loving heart.

To foster forgiveness, including loving-kindness and compassion, we could start by thinking of all people as members of our own family – recognizing that they all share our desire to be happy and free from suffering. We all share the same basic feelings, desires and goals.

For forgiveness to start taking root, we need to pause here to contemplate this truth, encapsulated as follows: "I feel compassion for all the beings who, like me, want to be happy and free from suffering" (Yongey Mingyur Rinpoche).

Finally, in view of the serious ramifications of unforgiveness – and the joy and well-being stemming from forgiveness – the many admonitions in the New Testament for cultivating a forgiving spirit can be fully appreciated. Here is a selection:

"See to it that no one misses the grace of God and that no bitter root grows up to cause trouble and defile many." (Hebrews 12:15)

"Forgive us our debts, as we also have forgiven our debtors. ... For if you forgive men when they sin against you, your heavenly Father will also forgive you. But if you do not forgive men their sins, your Father will not forgive your sins." (Matthew 6:12-15)

"And when you stand praying, if you hold anything against anyone, forgive him, so that your Father in heaven may forgive you your sins." (Mark 11:25)

"Bear with each other and forgive whatever grievances you may have against one another. Forgive as the Lord forgave you." (Colossians 3:13)

"So watch yourselves. If your brother sins, rebuke him, and if he repents, forgive him. If he sins against you seven times in a day, and seven times comes back to you and says, 'I repent,' forgive him." (Luke 17:3-4)

"Jesus said, 'Father, forgive them, for they do not know what they are doing.'" (Luke 23:34)

"If we confess our sins, he is faithful and just and will forgive us our sins and purify us from all unrighteousness." (1 John 1:9)

The Peace Method

In the suffering of loss through a scam, you may wonder whether you will ever be able to enjoy peace of mind again. The trauma of the scam may continue for some time to be viscerally real as some of the despair, grief, anger, guilt, and depression are still lingering.

In her book, *Grief Relief in 30 Minutes: How to Use the Peace Method to Go from Heartbreak to Happiness*, Aurora Winter describes the "Peace Method" which she formulated as a result of her own dealing with loss and grief in the untimely death of her husband. The Method consists of five steps to help release grief and get unstuck in loss.

The Peace Method methodically invites shifts of perception. It can thus alchemize pain into peace. The steps are:

P = Present Moment
E = Expressing Feelings
A = Acceptance and Appreciation
C = Considering the Contrary
E = Enthusiasm

Present Moment

The "P" stands for Present. It reminds us to begin healing by coming into the present moment.

Take a few deep breaths and get centered. (Just a few deep breaths can make a substantial difference. If you have more time, meditate for fifteen minutes, such as following the inflow and outflow of your breath.)

Notice if the perceived problem is in the present, past or future. We can never go back and change the past or solve all potential future problems. But we can deal with the one problem that is right here, right now. Additionally, problems may be validly seen as opportunities in disguise. The key is to take time to discover the opportunity.

Expressing Feelings

The "E" stands for *Express Your Feelings*. If you can't feel it, you can't heal it. Therefore give yourself and others full permission to vent.

Share with a trusted friend or family member your fears, worries, concerns and upset feelings. Or express your feelings in a journal, or a computer file. It is a gift to have a safe space to fully express your feelings and be understood before going on to any problem-solving activity.

Acceptance and Appreciation

The "A" stands for *Acceptance and / or Appreciation*. Stress is caused by resisting what is. When you resist reality, you will continue to feel like a victim. The past is not going to change, no matter how much you think it "should" be different. When you are resisting what is, you are not empowered.

Acceptance is the opposite of denial. It means that you make allowance for the reality of the current situation, but it does not mean you take no action. Acceptance empowers you to discover the best possible response.

Appreciation takes Acceptance even deeper. When you are able to discover something to appreciate, your sense of being victimized evaporates, and new possibilities emerge.

Considering the Contrary

The "C" stands for *Consider the Contrary*, or for rising to the *Challenge*. If you are suffering, consider the contrary of your painful thought.

Our minds work like a Google search. If you type "black" into Google, it is going to give you thousands of results for "black." When you type "white", it will give you thousands of results for "white."

In a similar way, when we think painful thoughts, our minds will find plenty of evidence, and we get to be right — and feel disempowered. When we consider the contrary and investigate peaceful or grateful thoughts, our minds will also find evidence, and we also get to be right — and become empowered.

You can also use the "C" as an invitation to rise to the challenge, and declare that you are going to meet and master the challenge before you.

Enthusiasm

The final "E" stands for Enthusiasm. This step invites you to make a conscious choice about an action to take, or a state of being to choose.

"Enthusiasm" comes from Latin and means "in God" – divinely inspired or filled with God. Choosing to be filled with God is like having a north star to guide you in the right direction. The meaning of the word also includes an activity or occupation pursued with intense interest.

This step invites you to take your eyes off the problem and look toward a solution. Choose something that you love doing, find fulfilling, consider important, or find inspiring. Set a vision and goal and move toward it. With enthusiasm, support will come from unexpected sources and breakthroughs will occur. To harness the power of enthusiasm, make sure your goal is connected to an activity, rather than a result. Enjoy the journey in the moment.

Loving One's Enemies

In the context of having been financially swindled by devious scammers, here is a unique reflection, based on various writings, that can help us see how to fulfill Jesus' command to love our enemies:

"But I say unto you, Love your enemies, bless them that curse you, do good to them that hate you, and pray for them which despitefully use you, and persecute you; ..." (Matthew 5:44, KJV)

"But love your enemies, do good, and lend, hoping for nothing in return; and your reward will be great, and you will be sons of the Most High. For He is kind to the unthankful and evil." (Luke 6:35, NKJV)

To have wealth and property is normally thought of as desirable, but attachment to them is an obstacle to our spiritual path.

The Bible cautions against "the love of money": "But godliness with contentment is great gain. For we brought nothing into the world, and we can take nothing out of it. But if we have food and clothing, we will be content with that. People who want to get rich fall into temptation and a trap and into many foolish and harmful desires that plunge men into ruin and destruction. For the love of money is a root of all kinds of evil. Some people, eager for money, have wandered from the faith and pierced themselves with many griefs." (1 Timothy 6:6-10)

Consequently, someone (such as a scammer) who deprives you of your money and/or possessions is, in fact, freeing you from the fetters these things could have created in your mind. Ideally, and this is certainly counter-intuitive, you can even feel gratitude.

If you own nothing, you are free. No enemies or thieves will bother you. As the saying goes: "If you have no wealth, thieves won't break in. If you carry no bags, robbers won't lie in wait."

It is also important to remember that a material loss may be the result of karma, or the law of compensation, coming into play. It could be the result of our having in some ways, even unwittingly, deprived others of their possessions in the past – though it may not be the case (karma is a complex issue). If it is the result of our past wrongdoing, then there is no reason to feel angry with anyone other than ourselves.

It is true that when we have money, we may attract dishonest people. In that sense we may become a target – and figuratively we may be shot at and suffer. Also, as a result of past negative actions, we may have set ourselves up as a target at which the arrows of suffering are now being shot. If we were not a target, there would be nothing at which to shoot arrows.

A truly spiritual person would ideally never have angry thoughts toward anyone who harms them. Instead, their main concern would be for the perpetrator's welfare. This is compassion, because the spiritual person knows that the scammers will have their turn at suffering in due time – when causes and conditions come together. (It sometimes seems that criminals get off scot-free – however, this is not the case in the long run, considering that life continues beyond death.)

To feel compassion for someone who has harmed us is an effective way of purifying our own shortcomings, freeing ourselves from anger, and developing the positive side of our nature. As a result, the harm that the person has done to us can help carry us along our spiritual path!

In the beginning, this may seem very difficult to put into practice. But to have a truly good heart is something for which everyone has the capacity – but it needs to be developed.

For example, consider doing this: Take all the suffering of the person harming you into your heart, and send them your own happiness, with great compassion.

For doing what is suggested above, it is important to have a thorough grounding in the practice of the four boundless attitudes. They are as follows:

-- boundless love, the wish that all others may have happiness;

-- boundless compassion, the wish that they may all be free from suffering;

-- boundless joy, the wish that all those who already have some happiness may keep and increase it; and

-- boundless impartiality, the recognition that beings are all equally deserving of love, compassion, and joy.

Finally, in the morning, our first thought should be the commitment to do whatever we can during the day to help others. If anyone has tried to harm us, make the wish that they be free from all animosity and vindictive feelings, and that all their positive aspirations may be fulfilled.

To bring about a true change in one's attitude in the way described is hard at first. However, if we understand the meaning behind this spiritual training, and keep on trying to apply it, we will find that it will help us in every difficult situation.

(Based on Rinpoche, Dilgo Khyentse. *The Heart of Compassion: The Thirty-Seven Verses on the Practice of a Bodhisattva*. Boulder, CO: Shambhala Publications, 2007.)

We are likely to feel anger towards someone who robs us or incites others to rob us. We may be saddened by having lost our possessions [money], besides which they have no right to deprive us of them. So we may decide to take the perpetrators to court to try to recover what we have lost. However, a spiritual person should not do such a thing. (Based on Dalai Lama, *Commentary on the Thirty-Seven Practices of a*

Bodhisattva. Dharamsala, India: Library of Tibetan Works and Archives, 1995.)

While in the world, we will definitely encounter adverse circumstances, for that is the nature of this world and to be expected. If we buckle under the pressure of stressful situations, it will be difficult to maintain, let alone advance our spiritual practice.

Therefore, we must transform unfavourable circumstances into our spiritual path, preparing us to enter the Kingdom of God. With help from beyond ourselves, we can transform distressing events and difficulties, as well as loss, ruin, suffering, blame, and criticism into the spiritual path.

If someone robs us of our wealth or possessions, or instructs others to, a spiritual person's response is not to retaliate.

When our money is stolen or things are ruined by others, it is helpful to remember that wealth and possessions can chain us to this world — they can make us overly preoccupied with worldly cares and concerns. So by stealing them, the thief, in a way, has broken some of those chains!

Also, when we have money and possessions, we can suffer from dissatisfaction, always wanting more and better. We can also worry about our money and possessions being stolen and feel the need to vigilantly protect them. In reality, however, clinging onto money and possessions with attachment, we create negative karma which will result in suffering.

Thinking in this way, we will see how the thief (scammer) has taken away some of the basis for our creating negative karma. They have actually released us from our chains and opened for us the door to true freedom.

Finally, because we are imperfect beings, in our past we have all accumulated some karma to suffer, and this is stored in our mind stream like money in a secure bank. By stealing our money and things, the thief has made some of that karma ripen so that now we are free of it. Unbelievable as it may sound, but based on the law of compensation, how kind they are to have robbed us of some of our bad karma! Obviously, this is very counter-intuitive!

Ideally, therefore, we should not see this person as an enemy, but as a friend who helps to free us from suffering. In this way, we can practice patience and develop compassion.

(Based on Geshe Jampa Tegchok, *Transforming Adversity into Joy and Courage: An Explanation of the Thirty-Seven Practices of Bodhisattvas*. Ithaca, NY: Snow Lion Publications, 2013.)

Prayers

Prayers for Ourselves and the Scammers

These prayers were written shortly after experiencing the scam.

Prayer for the Scammers (and Ourselves)

Dear Heavenly Father,

While I am going through waves of not feeling well and being heavy-hearted, I pray for Veronica and her accomplices who took our money. I pray that they can swiftly see that a life of crime is not going to help them in the long run, certainly not in the next world – because there are definite consequences involving suffering. I pray that they can come to heartfelt regret and remorse over their actions and that they will change their ways while they can.

I pray for other people who have been scammed and lost much more than us. We are not alone in this. I pray not just for ourselves to retrieve our money, but especially for those who have lost far more of their savings and are now greatly hurting. Despite our financial setback, there is still much to be grateful for.

I don't quite understand why I am feeling bad and hurting – perhaps it is a form of grief and hurt since we have experienced a loss. Thank you, however, for the understanding we now have about how clever and devious manipulation works and how we can all potentially become victims.

I pray for ourselves to heal and be able to go on – and for a good outcome, both for ourselves and those involved. I pray for forgiveness of any unethical behaviour that I have even unknowingly committed, and I forgive all the perpetrators of this scam crime against us. I really don't feel hate or even anger toward them.

I pray that the bank will be able to recover our money and restore it to our account. I pray for peace and calmness. Again, I am deeply grateful that our loss was not worse – and for the wonderful mercy that we have been shown.

I pray that Veronica is influenced from beyond by loving heavenly beings in a positive way, and that she is open to this influence. May she change her ways before it is too late in her life.

May it be so – Amen.

Prayer for Ourselves (and Others)

Dear Heavenly Father,

We have been unwittingly conned, deceived and robbed – unfortunately and ironically with our own cooperation. It has affected us deeply and we need healing of our hearts and minds.

Despite our financial loss, we are grateful that we didn't suffer a far greater setback, such as having all our savings mercilessly taken away. We pray for those who have been scammed out of their life or retirement savings – and we pray for the scammers that they will be dealt with mercifully. Both the scammers and their victims need help and compassion.

We don't know why this financial scam has beset us – it all occurred so swiftly. It is uncanny that we both did not catch on earlier in the process of being deceived.

Nonetheless, we are already gaining insights and learning lessons. We will certainly be more circumspect and careful from now on. Perhaps we were naïve and far too trusting of people we did not know and who were only first-time contacts online. It is amazing and hard to believe, just how we were manipulated step by step into compliance.

You promise that all things work together for good, and that we will not be tested beyond our abilities. The latter has certainly been the case – and we deeply believe the former as well. We are getting a far more compassionate understanding of how the world operates and the evil that abounds – and how urgently we need to pray "Your Kingdom come."

We remain hopeful that some or all of the money will be recovered. In the meantime, we are grateful that it was not a far worse setback.

May we focus on the many, many good things and the blessings in our lives and not on this issue – even though we feel violated, taken advantage of, betrayed, and perhaps somewhat angry.

Help us to remember – and be deeply grateful – that we were recently protected from three near-accidents that we know of. For some reason we were not protected from this situation, but almost led into it. It is so puzzling, but perhaps there is a purpose working out.

We pray for healing for ourselves, as well as forgiveness and compassion for the perpetrators. More importantly, we pray for others that have been scammed in excruciating ways.

Finally, may the law enforcement agencies be blessed in their work of dealing with all types of scam situations – that are sadly abounding more and more.

Amen – may it be so.

Prayer from a Different Perspective

Earlier this year, one of the most influential Zen masters of our time, Thich Nhat Hanh, departed his physical body at age 96. Here is some of his advice on the "right way to pray."

"If you are standing on one shore and want to cross over to the other shore, you have to use a boat or swim across. You cannot just pray, 'Oh, other shore, please come over here for me to step across!'

To a Buddhist, praying without also practicing is not real prayer. In a real prayer, you ask only for the things you really need, things that are necessary for your well-being, such as peace, solidity, and freedom – freedom from anger, fear and craving. Happiness and well-being are not possible without peace, solidity and freedom. Most of our desires are not for our peace, solidity and freedom.

While you pray, you are deeply aware of what you really need and what is just the object of your desire. This kind of prayer is the light of God that shines upon you, telling you which way to go in order to obtain peace, solidity and freedom. In a real prayer, you also touch the wholesome seeds in your consciousness and water them. These are seeds of compassion, love, understanding, forgiveness and joy. If while praying you can recognize these seeds in you and help them grow, your prayer is already a deep practice."

Below is a Buddhist prayer for love and compassion that embodies Thich Nhat Hanh's words above.

The Nine Prayers
May I be peaceful, happy, and light in body and spirit.
May I be free from injury. May I live in safety.
May I be free from disturbance, fear, anxiety, and worry.

May I learn to look at myself with the eyes of understanding and love.

May I be able to recognize and touch the seeds of joy and happiness in myself.

May I learn to identify and see the sources of anger, craving, and delusion in myself.

May I know how to nourish the seeds of joy in myself every day.

May I be able to live fresh, solid, and free.

May I be free from attachment and aversion, but not be indifferent.

Source: https://www.stillnessspeaks.com/nine-prayers-thich-nhat-hanh/

Afterword

I would like to end this book with the following thoughts and a Bible promise that has been remarkably fulfilled.

Despite the setback and initial trauma, our story shows that a trial can indeed work for the good and bring about spiritual growth that would otherwise not have occurred.

As Aurora Winter advises in her Peace Method (described earlier in this book), why not consider the contrary of the initial feelings and emotions? Why not appreciate the good parts of what happened, rather than focusing on the worst of it? Why not be grateful that the trial was not worse, but rather was tempered by mercy? Why not keep reminding ourselves of the blessings of life and be grateful for them all?

Once we consider the suffering and plight of so many in the world, our problem, whatever it may be in each case, will look at worst comparable to what others are going through as a part of our shared earthly existence. But more likely, our issues will appear small, or even insignificant, in comparison. Rather than feeling sorry for ourselves, we can start feeling compassion for others and look for ways to make their heavy burdens more bearable. This can start with prayer, and if feasible, include physical or financial help.

Afterword

I am certain that our prayer shortly after being scammed has been answered. It included the following quoted reflections and requests:

"[The scam] has affected us deeply and we need healing of our hearts and feelings."

We can honestly say, that we have received a healing in that the hurtful emotions have subsided and we are able to move on with life. There may still be occasional triggers or flashbacks, but overall, we feel much better. We can also see the good that has come out of the experience, mostly wisdom and spiritual growth.

"We are uncertain why it had happened; it was all so uncanny that we both didn't catch on earlier. But there are already lessons and insights."

A new perspective we have gained is that there was a purpose for it and good has come out of it. Our insights have resulted in this book and a website with similar information that my husband has created. We hope that both sources of information will help others – those who have been scammed, and those who are working through other losses and hardships.

"It is amazing and hard to believe, just how we were manipulated into compliance. You [Father] promise that all things work together for good, and that we won't be tested beyond our abilities. The latter has certainly been the case and the former as well. Perhaps we are getting a more compassionate understanding about how the world operates and the evil that abounds."

This is still very true – both the good that has come from the experience in terms of learning and spiritual growth, and the fact that while difficult, the situation was not unbearable. The cover picture is symbolic of our journey from darkness to light, from a dark night through dawn to sunrise on a new day.

"Help us to remember and be grateful that we were protected from three near-accidents that we know of. For some reason we were not protected from this situation, but almost led into it. It is so puzzling, but perhaps there is a purpose working out."

One of the purposes we see is sharing the information in this book with others to help ease their burdens. Our experience indeed shows that while we were scammed, we were clearly protected from a far worse situation, and we remain immensely grateful for that. In the overall scheme of things, especially considering the afterlife into which we cannot take any of our earthly possessions, this scam loss is of minor significance.

"We pray for healing for ourselves, forgiveness for the perpetrators, as well as compassion. Compassion is especially needed for others that have been scammed in a far more painful way, as this is a very common problem and becoming more so."

I do not feel anger or hate for the perpetrators, and certainly have more compassion for those who are

Afterword

losing money through scams – but, more importantly, also those who have lost belongings, and even loved ones, through earthquakes, floods, fires, wars, terrorism, crime, accidents, and the many other tragedies that are a part of this dark, sad world.

To end on a positive and hopeful note, I believe that this world is going, and will continue to go, through a transition and transformation into a better world. It may well go through yet greater darkness, before the dawn comes and the sun rises. But, as with other civilizations before ours, there will not be a permanent end and annihilation. I believe that a remnant of humanity will survive whatever catastrophes – man-made, natural or supernatural – may be ahead. Such events tend to cause people to consider higher realities and seek help from Beyond. Some of the survivors will have learned important lessons and be able to lead others into a better world based on love and harmony.

I also believe that this world is not all there is. There is an afterlife, where the situation that each of us will find ourselves in will depend on how we lived in this life. Because of the law of cause and effect, if we have done well, we will enter a realm of joy and happiness. If we have lived in an unwholesome way, there will be penalties to be paid – but then also opportunities for progression from darkness to light. No one is destined for everlasting punishment in hell, but all will have opportunities to reach a place of happiness. We are the architects of our future reality.

So whatever challenges and trials we encounter during this short and fleeting earthly existence, each can be seen as a bump in the road, a possible detour, a learning experience – all a training for what is going to be a far more lasting reality. In the overall scheme of things, as time goes on, what seemed like a big deal or major drama at the time will fade into near insignificance.

I would like to end with a scripture that I find most encouraging: "We know that in all things God works for the good of those who love him, who have been called according to his purpose. (Romans 8:28)

If we can believe this, and look for the good in each trial and setback, we will be able to give thanks as we see the fulfillment of this universal promise in our lives.

> I can see clearly now the rain is gone
> I can see all obstacles in my way
> Gone are the dark clouds that had me blind ...
> Oh, yes I can make it now the pain is gone
> All of the bad feelings have disappeared
> Here is the rainbow I've been praying for
> It's gonna be a bright (bright)
> Bright (bright) sunshiny day
>
> (Song by Jimmy Cliff)

About the Authors

Eva Peck

Eva Peck has an international and Christian background. Having lived and worked in Australia, the United States, Europe, Asia, and the Middle East, including teaching English as a foreign language, she has experienced a range of cultures, customs, and environments and spiritual traditions. She now draws on those experiences in her writing.

Eva has a Bachelor's degree in Biological Sciences, a post-graduate Diploma in Education, and a Master's degree in Theology.

She is interested in nature, spirituality and writing – bringing together information to educate and edify others and help them on their spiritual journey.

Eva lives in Brisbane, Australia, with her husband, Alex and their cat Whitey.

Alexander Peck

Three overarching themes emerge as Alexander looks at the landscape of his life: education, writing and spirituality.

After finishing high school in Australia, he entered Teacher's College and received elementary school teaching credentials. In his third and final year, he specialized in school librarianship. Later, while living and working in the United States, he completed a Masters in Education, with an emphasis in instructional design, at California State University in Long Beach.

Apart from a few years of teaching, during most of his career, Alexander was engaged in writing – involving research, compiling information, editing, documentation writing, educational writing, and website creation.

Alexander's life-long passion has been spirituality. After Teacher's College, he went abroad to pursue a Bachelor of Arts degree with an emphasis in theology, starting in England, and completing his degree in Pasadena, California.

While teaching English as a foreign language to first-year university students in South Korea, Alexander pursued PhD studies in Christian Education at Hoseo University, a private Christian school in Cheonan City. He completed all the course work and passed the qualifying exams. However, due to circumstances at the time, he was unable to complete his dissertation on the topic of "The Spirituality of John Amos Comenius." (Comenius was a Moravian philosopher, pedagogue, and theologian, and is considered the father of modern education.)

Between 2007 and 2010, Alexander completed two Master's degrees through distance education with the University of Newcastle in New South Wales, Australia – one with a theology emphasis, the other specializing in Christian spirituality.

Late in 2011, he encountered Buddhism through the teachings of Father Laurence Freeman OSB, a Catholic priest and Benedictine monk. In a series of talks, Father Freeman quoted from *Dhammapada*. It was the spirituality of this collection of the Buddha's sayings, and other Buddhist writings, that caught Alexander's attention. He followed up with further Buddhist study for over a decade until the present time.

Now in his seventies, Alexander values quiet and peaceful lifestyle with his wife, Eva, and their adorable white cat, Whitey, on the bay side of Brisbane, Australia. He cherishes having time for sharing spirituality insights via his writing and websites.

About Pathway Publishing

Pathway Publishing is dedicated to sharing truth and beauty by publishing books and producing websites that present what is true to life and reality, as well as what is lovely and inspirational. The goal is to not only provide sound information, but also to uplift the human spirit.

Pathway Publishing has a vision of enriching the life of readers here and now, as well as helping them on their path of enlightenment and spiritual transformation. The wisdom and experience of spiritual teachers, thinkers, and visionary writers from various backgrounds and faith traditions are recognized and valued.

Books produced by Pathway Publishing broadly fall into two categories – spirituality and the arts – and include:

- *Divine Reflections in Times and Seasons*, Eva Peck
- *Divine Reflections in Natural Phenomena*, Eva Peck
- *Divine Reflections in Living Things*, Eva Peck
- *Divine Insights from Human Life,* Eva Peck
- *Pathway to Life - Through the Holy Scriptures,* Eva and Alexander Peck
- *Journey to the Divine Within – Through Silence, Stillness and Simplicity,* Alexander and Eva Peck
- *Jesus' Gospel of God's Love*, Eva Peck

- *New Birth – Pathway to the Kingdom of God*, Eva Peck
- *Gospel of God's Grace and His Kingdom – Insights and Reflections*, Eva Peck
- *Abundant Living on Small Income*, Eva Peck
- *The Greatest Love*, Eva Peck
- *Salvation*, Eva Peck
- *Problem of Evil*, Eva Peck
- *Answers to Prayer*, Eva Peck
- *The Bible as a Guide to Life*, Eva Peck
- *Life After Death*, Eva Peck
- *Jesus Christ – A New Look at His Identity and Mission*, Eva Peck and Michael Nedbal
- *Fulfillments of Old Testament Types*, Eva Peck
- *Nature of Soul and Spirit*, Eva Peck
- *Discerning Truth and Divine Guidance*, Eva Peck
- *Antidote to Fear and Anxiety – Fear of God*, Eva Peck

- *Artistic Inspirations - Paintings of Jindrich Degen* arranged by Eva and Alexander Peck
- *Colour and Contrast – Artwork of Jindrich Degen* arranged by Eva and Alexander Peck
- *Faces and Forms Across Time – Artwork of Jindrich Degen*, arranged by Eva and Alexander Peck
- *Variations – Art Exhibition of Jindrich Degen*, arranged by Eva and Alex Peck
- *Floral and Nature Art – Photography of Jindrich Degen,* arranged by Eva and Alexander Peck

- *Nature's Beauty – Art Photography of Jindrich Degen*, arranged by Eva and Alex Peck

- *Volné verše,* Jindrich Degen (Czech poetry)
- *Verše pro dnešní dobu,* Jindrich Degen (Czech poetry)
- *Pardál za úplňku a jiné povídky,* Eva Vaníčková (Czech stories set mostly in Indonesia)

http://www.pathway-publishing.org/

Pathway Publishing
Seeking truth and beauty

www.ingramcontent.com/pod-product-compliance
Lightning Source LLC
Chambersburg PA
CBHW031425290426
44110CB00011B/528